discovermore

Transportation

# Focus on Ships

Doug Bradley



Britannica
Educational Publishing
IN ASSOCIATION WITH
THE ROSEN PUBLISHING GROUP

Published in 2026 by Britannica Educational Publishing (a trademark of Encyclopædia Britannica, Inc.)
in association with The Rosen Publishing Group, Inc.
2544 Clinton Street, Buffalo, NY 14224



Distributed exclusively by Rosen Publishing.
To see additional Britannica Educational Publishing titles, go to rosenpublishing.com.



Editor: Greg Roza
Book Design: Michael Flynn

Photo Credits: Cover NAN728/Shutterstock.com; (series background) Dai Yim/Shutterstock.com; p. 4 VladSV/Shutterstock.com; p. 5 Michael Dechev/Shutterstock.com; p. 6 shaineast/Shutterstock.com; p. 7 Fotos593/Shutterstock.com; p. 8 Kokhanchikov/Shutterstock.com; p. 9 https://en.wikipedia.org/wiki/File:Battle_of_Scheveningen_(Slag_bij_Ter_Heijde)(Jan_Abrahamsz._Beerstraten).jpg; p. 10 https://commons.wikimedia.org/wiki/File:The_Monitor_and_Merrimac.jpg; p. 11 Igor Hotinsky/Shutterstock.com; p. 12 bogdan ionescu/Shutterstock.com; p. 13 CANARAN/Shutterstock.com; p. 14 Matthew James Ferguson/Shutterstock.com; p. 15 https://commons.wikimedia.org/wiki/File:"Seawise_Giant"_-_Singapore,_1990.jpg; pp. 16, 21 (top) GreenOak/Shutterstock.com; p. 17 Sven Hansche/Shutterstock.com; p. 19 (top) Jordan Lye/Shutterstock.com; p. 19 (bottom) Edgar Lee Espe/Shutterstock.com; p. 21 (bottom) Vytautas Kielaitis/Shutterstock.com; p. 22 https://commons.wikimedia.org/wiki/File:US_Navy_040730-N-1234E-002_PCU_Virginia_(SSN_774)_returns_to_the_General_Dynamics_Electric_Boat_shipyard.jpg; p. 23 EvgeniiAnd/Shutterstock.com; p. 24 https://commons.wikimedia.org/wiki/File:RMS_Titanic_2.jpg; p. 25 Wayleebird/Shutterstock.com; p. 26 Adwo/Shutterstock.com; p. 27 maks_ph/Shutterstock.com; p. 28 Travel mania/Shutterstock.com; p. 29 Dipix/Shutterstock.com.

Cataloging-in-Publication Data

Names: Bradley, Doug, 1971-.
Title: Focus on ships / Doug Bradley.
Description: New York : Britannica Educational Publishing, in association with Rosen Educational Services, 2026. | Series: Discover more: transportation | Includes glossary and index.
Identifiers: ISBN 9781641905510 (library bound) | ISBN 9781641905503 (pbk) | ISBN 9781641905527 (ebook)
Subjects: LCSH: Ships--Juvenile literature. | Shipping--Juvenile literature.
Classification: LCC VM150.B697 2026 | DDC 623.82--dc23

Manufactured in the United States of America



CPSIA Compliance Information: Batch #CWBRIT26. For further information contact Rosen Publishing at 1-800-237-9932.

# Contents


Let's Get Moving! .......................... 4
A Closer Look at Ships.................... 6
The History of Boats ...................... 8
Moving Cargo...............................12
Tanker Ships................................14
Container Ships............................16
Industrial and Factory Ships............18
In the Military ...........................20
Vacationing at Sea ........................24
Specialty Transport Ships...............26
Sailing into the Future ..................28
*Glossary* ....................................30
*For More Information* ...................31
*Index* ........................................32

# Let's Get Moving!

Transportation is the movement of people, animals, and goods from one place to another. This is happening constantly all over the world. Since almost 75 percent of Earth's surface is covered by water, ships do a lot of this work. Ships are large boats that can carry passengers or cargo for long distances over water.

Many of the products you buy online and in stores were transported by container ship.

Commercial ships move about 11 billion tons of cargo every year!

Before the invention of the airplane, crossing oceans and large bodies of water could only be done by ship. Although there is faster transportation now, ships are as important today as they have ever been. Food, wood, and minerals are taken from farms, forests, and mines to factories around the world. There, they are used to make millions of products ranging from anvils to zippers. These new manufactured goods are then shipped around the world. Large cargo vessels may take weeks or even months to reach their destinations.

## Consider This

Airplanes now ship cargo all over the world too. Why would a company chose to use cargo ships rather than cargo airplanes to send their products overseas?

# A Closer Look at Ships

The front of a ship is called the bow. The back is the stern. A ship's left side is known as the port side. The right is the starboard side. A ship's frame, or body, is called the hull. The keel is like the ship's backbone. It keeps the ship from tipping over. A rudder is a flat panel that is moved from side to side to provide steering control.

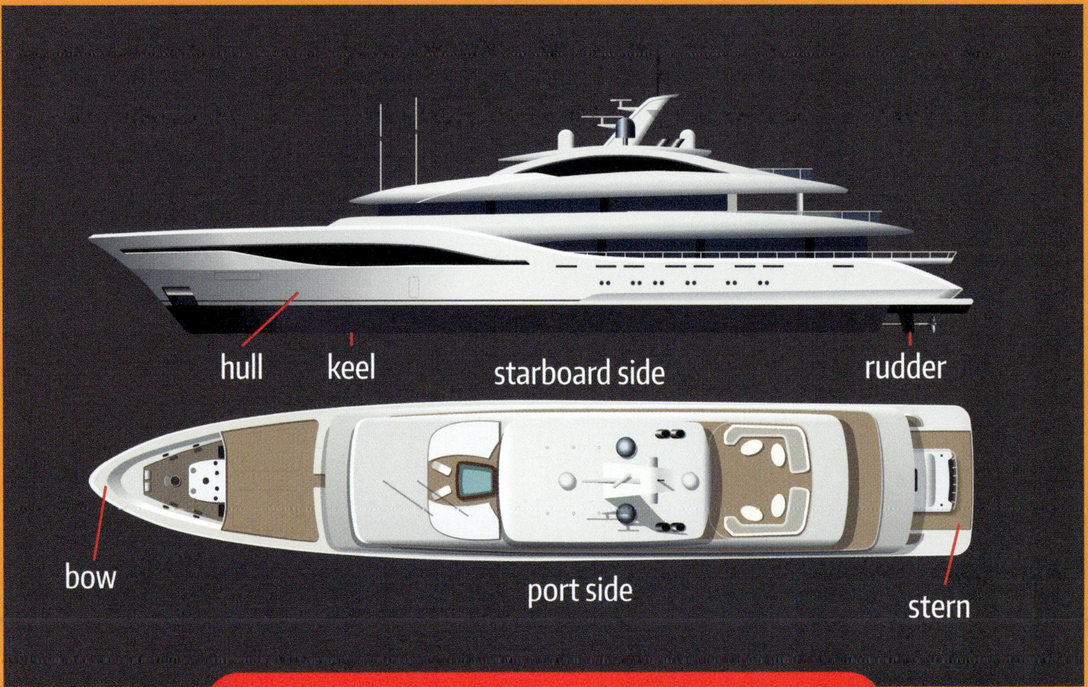


These are the basic parts that all ships have.

The control rooms in large cargo ships are high up and give the crew a clear view of their surroundings.

Ships usually have many decks. The decks are like the floors of a building. Cabins for passengers, engine and control rooms, and spaces for cargo are often on different decks. An engine inside the ship provides energy to propellers at the back of the ship. The propellers **propel** the ship through the water. When the ship is not moving, a heavy metal anchor may be lowered into the water to keep the ship in place.

## WORD WISE

PROPEL MEANS TO TO PUSH OR DRIVE SOMETHING FORWARD OR ONWARD.

# The History of Boats

The first boats, called canoes, were carved from trees. At first, people used their hands to move their canoes through the water. Eventually, wooden oars were used instead of hands.

Later, people attached sails made of cloth to **masts** on their boats. This allowed them to use the wind to power bigger boats through the water. These bigger boats were the first ships. Using sail and oar power together allowed these ships to move faster.

This carving in an Egyptian temple shows how important ships were to the ancient Egyptians.

Aside from trade, ships were also used for exploration and war.

By the 1400s ships began to carry as many as three masts. Christopher Columbus, Vasco da Gama, and other explorers used ships like this to reach unexplored territory. When new lands were found, settlers moved there on ships. Once travel between countries became easier, trade increased. This in turn led to larger cargo ships.

## WORD WISE

**A MAST IS A LONG POLE THAT RISES FROM THE BOTTOM OF A SHIP OR BOAT AND SUPPORTS THE SAILS AND RIGGING. THE BIGGER THE SHIP, THE MORE MASTS IT GENERALLY HAS.**

For hundreds of years, ships were made mainly of wood. Wood was a plentiful resource. Then, a big change came to ship design. In the 1800s iron began to replace wood as the most popular shipbuilding material. It was stronger and made it possible to build larger ships that could carry more goods.

Early iron warships were called ironclads. They were powered by steam. The first battle between ironclads took place between the North (USS *Merrimack*) and South (CSS *Virginia*) during the American Civil War.

Ship engine rooms are filled with highly technical equipment! Ships need highly trained workers to keep them working properly.

Iron was also used to build the mighty steamboats that replaced sailing ships. The first steam engines ran on coal. The engines became smaller as time went on, leaving more room for cargo. These improvements had an important effect on trade around the world.

Today most modern ship engines are powered by oil. Others use coal or nuclear energy. Thanks to modern engines, a ship can now cross an ocean in a few days instead of a few weeks.

## Consider This

Why are engines more reliable than sails for powering a ship?

# Moving Cargo

The ancient Egyptians were the first people to build cargo ships. They carried trading cargo as well as huge pieces of stone. The stones were used to construct buildings and monuments. Today, cargo ships carry much more.

Before the steam engine was invented, ancient vessels were powered by sails and by humans using oars.

Some roll-on/roll-off ships are so big that tractor trailers can drive right into them!

Cargo ships carry almost anything that can fit in boxes, crates, bales, and barrels. They also carry products that are hard to ship in containers, such as coal, grain, steel, lumber, and farm products. Some cargo ships can even carry small numbers of passengers.

There are several types of cargo ships. One type is known as a roll-on/roll-off ship. These ships have large ramps at the bow or stern that allow vehicles to be driven on and off cargo ships for transport. This saves hours of loading and unloading time. Tankers and container ships are two of the largest kinds of cargo ships.

## Consider This

The largest container ships today are about 1,300 feet (400 m) long. On a ship that big, do you think you can feel the movement of the ocean?

# Tanker Ships

Tankers have many tanks used to transport liquids, such as oil and chemicals. If one tank fails, the rest remain safe. Most tanks are contained in the bottom of the ship. Oil tankers carry oil, which is taken to refineries, where it is used to make gasoline, diesel fuel, and heating oil. These new products are loaded into new tankers and taken around the world. Tankers also carry less dangerous liquids such as orange juice and vegetable oil.

Oil tankers carry oil all around the world. This one is heading for San Francisco, California.

The largest supertanker ever was the *Knock Nevis*, or *Seaward Giant*. At 1,503 feet (458 m), it was longer than the Empire State Building is tall!

Modern tankers can transport ten times more than ships could fifty years ago. This increase in **capacity** means larger ships and larger risk. Chemicals must be transported in special tanks lined with protective coatings. A tank's inside coating depends on the liquid being transported. Any spill from a supertanker could seriously damage the environment or hurt people.

## WORD WISE

**CAPACITY IS THE LARGEST AMOUNT OR NUMBER THAT CAN BE CONTAINED IN SOMETHING.**

# Container Ships

You've likely seen cargo containers being pulled by trucks on the highway. They are large boxes made of metal. They come in several lengths, but they all have the same width so they can be stacked and transported easily. They hold goods that have been manufactured and are ready to sell. Container ships can carry food, televisions, clothing, and more. Containers are stored above deck as well as below. Megaships can carry more than 24,000 containers.

Shipping containers can be between 20 feet (6.1 m) and 53 feet (16.2 m) long. However they are all 8 feet (2.4 m) wide so they can be safely stacked on container ships.

Shippers must keep track of every container for the system to work. They do this by labelling each container and checking when it departs and arrives. Some shippers track their containers electronically. When ships pull in to port, the containers are removed by a **crane**. The containers are taken from there by trucks or trains.

## WORD WISE

**A CRANE IS A MACHINE WITH A SWINGING ARM FOR LIFTING AND CARRYING HEAVY LOADS.**

# Industrial and Factory Ships

Some ships are designed for industrial processes while at sea. Some industrial ships are also factory ships. As the name suggests, these ships are like factories at sea. For instance, fish factories are ships that work out in the ocean with a fleet of large fishing ships. As ships catch fish, they pull alongside a factory ship. The factory ship processes and freezes the fish. Once loaded, it can be taken directly to shore for sale.

Some industrial ships do not go anywhere for a long time. For example, deep-sea oil rigs are placed in one spot to pump oil from the ocean floor. They have crews that work, eat, and sleep on board. Some industrial ships burn hazardous waste far at sea.

Some fishing ships are floating factories!

## compare and contrast

How are oil rigs out at sea different from those built on land? How are they similar? Could one replace the other?

Oil rigs are truly gigantic! They can be towed to different locations if necessary.

# In the Military

Many countries have a navy to help defend themselves. A navy is the branch of a country's armed forces that fights on, under, or over the sea. There are many different types of ships that navies use. Some military ships are used to transport soldiers, sailors, and their equipment around the world.

Aircraft carriers are the largest military ships. They can carry up to one hundred aircraft that can take off and land on the ship. It takes hundreds of men and women to keep an aircraft carrier afloat. Cruisers, destroyers, and frigates are all much smaller than aircraft carriers. They protect carriers against attack and launch missiles and torpedoes. Many navies have ships that perform a small number of jobs. Hospital ships are floating hospitals. Helicopters transport patients to and from hospital ships.

Aircraft carriers are called cities at sea. That's because they are at sea for months at a time, and need hairdressers, cooks, store clerks, and many other types of workers.

## compare and contrast

How is the top deck of an aircraft carrier different from other military ships? Why do you think that is?

Destroyers help keep aircraft carriers from being attacked.

Submarines, or subs, are underwater ships. They can stay underwater for months. They don't even need to come to the surface for fuel and supplies. They patrol the sea and can launch torpedoes during wartime. They have tanks that are filled with air to make the ship rise or water to make it dive down into the ocean. Pushing the water out of the tanks helps these ships rise to the surface.

Some military submarines can stay beneath the surface for months at a time.

Military subs can carry about 150 sailors and can stay underwater for months. They must carry plenty of food, as well as cooks to prepare meals.

Submarines are also used by scientists to explore the deepest parts of oceans. Scientific researchers and explorers usually use smaller submarines. These submarines may have mechanical arms, cameras, and other tools to help scientists study the underwater world.

## Consider This

The British sub HMS *Artful* has a nuclear engine that won't need to be refueled for 25 years! That means it can stay underwater up to a quarter century. Can you think of a reason why the ship would need to come up to the surface?

# Vacationing at Sea

Passenger ships, also called ocean liners, are massive ships that carry large numbers of tourists, or people who are traveling for fun. They were very popular before airplanes made it possible to travel far distances in a short time. By the 1960s these ships could make the trip from America to England in four days.

The RMS *Titanic* was a British passenger ship that hit an iceberg and sunk on April 5, 1912. Safety measures have improved greatly since that time.

The largest class of passenger ship if the *Oasis* class. They have many restaurants, stores, and theaters. They also have water parks, ziplines, and other exciting attractions. Some passenger ships even have roller coasters!

Though not as common, passenger ships are still in use today. They don't travel as fast as they used to, but they use less energy than airplanes. Most trips across the Atlantic Ocean take about seven or eight days and are designed for enjoyment.

Modern ocean liners are called cruise ships, and they can be enormous. Some are almost as long as supertankers. They transport thousands of passengers. They have dining rooms and cabins for guests to sleep. Many cruise ships feature exercise rooms, swimming pools, and shopping. Travelers also get to see live shows from famous performers.

## Consider This

Airplane travel is much faster than ocean travel. If that's true, why would anyone sail to their destination?

# Specialty Transport Ships

Some transport ships are used for a specific, or single, job. Cable ships lay and repair underwater cable on the ocean floor. Underwater cables are used for **telecommunication**, for electric power, or for other purposes. These ships help keep the world connected. Livestock carriers move sheep, cattle, and other animals from one place to another.

Livestock ships in warm areas, such as this one, are "open-air" ships so the animals can breathe fresh air.

Icebreaking ships have an extra layer of steel to make a path through frozen waters for other ships.

Icebreakers are ships that clear a path through frozen water for scientific ships and other vessels. Some are military ships operated by the U.S. Navy and Coast Guard. Research ships are smaller ships that carry scientists who conduct research at sea. Research ships often have laboratories on board. Some research ships are used to look for oil. Some allow scientists to study sea creatures in their environment.

## WORD WISE

**TELECOMMUNICATION IS ANY KIND OF HUMAN COMMUNICATION THAT TAKES PLACE ACROSS A DISTANCE.**

# Sailing into the Future

Today, tens of thousands of ships of all sorts move cargo and passengers around the world. The world's merchant **fleet** is huge. Nine out of every ten pounds of goods on our planet are transported by ship. Since thousands of ships are involved, international agreements and uniform industry practices are needed to maintain an orderly flow of commerce.

As the population of the world increases, more ships will be built to carry more goods to more people.

Egypt's Suez Canal enables ships to travel between Europe and Asia without going around Africa.

Ship technology will continue to improve. The future of shipping may include ghost ships, or ships that are controlled by a captain on land. The captain will be able to navigate the ship based on data that is received from the ship's sensors. Can you think of any other future improvements we might see in ship and shipping technology?

## WORD WISE

**A FLEET IS A GROUP OF SHIPS SAILING TOGETHER, ENGAGED IN THE SAME ACTIVITY, OR UNDER THE SAME OWNERSHIP.**

# Glossary

**anchor** A device usually of metal that is attached to a boat or ship by a cable and that when thrown overboard holds the boat or ship in place.

**bow** The front end of a ship.

**captain** The officer in charge of a ship.

**cargo** The goods transported in a ship.

**craft** A small boat.

**deck** The floor of a ship.

**freight** Goods or cargo carried by ship, train, truck, or airplane.

**hull** The frame or body of a ship.

**keel** A timber or plate running lengthwise along the center of the bottom of a ship and usually sticking out from the bottom.

**merchant** Relating to trade. A merchant ship carries people or cargo for a fee.

**oar** A long pole with a broad blade at one end, used for rowing or steering a boat.

**port** The left side of a ship (looking forward).

**propeller** A device consisting of a hub fitted with blades that is made to turn rapidly by an engine and is used especially for propelling airplanes and ships.

**rigging** The ropes and chains used aboard a ship that control the sails and supporting masts.

**rudder** A flat movable piece (as of wood or metal) attached to the rear of a ship or aircraft for steering.

**starboard** The right side of a ship (looking forward).

**stern** The rear end of a boat.

**submarine** A vessel designed to operate underwater.

**vessel** A craft larger than a rowboat that is used for transportation on water.

# For More Information

## Books

Crestodina, Tom. *Working Boats: An Inside Look at Ten Amazing Watercraft.* Seattle, WA: Little Bigfoot, 2022.

Marlin, Charles. *Ships (Military Machines).* Burnsville, MN: North Star Editions, 2025.

## Websites

**Container Ship Facts for Kids**
*kids.kiddle.co/Container_ship*
Read more about container ships here.

**Titanic**
*kids.britannica.com/kids/article/Titanic/353863*
Learn about the tragic sinking of the RMS *Titanic* with Britannica Kids.

Publisher's note to educators and parents: Our editors have carefully reviewed these websites to ensure that they are suitable for students. Many websites change frequently, however, and we cannot guarantee that a site's future contents will continue to meet our high standards of quality and educational value. Be advised that students should be closely supervised whenever they access the internet.

# Index


## A
anchor, 7

## C
cargo, 4, 5, 7, 9, 11, 12, 13, 16, 28
container ships, 4, 13, 16, 17
control room, 7

## D
decks, 5, 16, 21

## E
engine, 7, 11, 23

## F
fishing ships, 18, 19

## I
industrial ships, 18, 19
ironclads, 10

## M
masts, 8, 9
military ships, 10, 20, 21, 22, 23, 27

## O
oars, 8, 12
oil rigs, 18, 19

## P
passengers, 4, 7, 13, 25, 28
passenger ships, 24, 25
propellers, 7

## R
RMS *Titanic*, 24

## S
sails, 8, 9, 11, 12
specialty transport ships, 26, 27
supertankers, 15, 25

## T
tanker ships, 13, 14, 15